How to Pray a Good Prayer and Simple Guide for Normal People and Get Answered (With Testimonies)

The Blessed Creation

Published by The Blessed Creation, 2023.

While every precaution has been taken in the preparation of this book, the publisher assumes no responsibility for errors or omissions, or for damages resulting from the use of the information contained herein.

HOW TO PRAY A GOOD PRAYER AND SIMPLE GUIDE FOR NORMAL PEOPLE AND GET ANSWERED (WITH TESTIMONIES)

First edition. February 21, 2023.

ISBN: 979-8215503805

Written by The Blessed Creation.

Also by The Blessed Creation

How to Pray a Good Prayer and Simple Guide for Normal People and
Get Answered (With Testimonies)
Panda Panda Bear What Do You Learn: With Jokes and Quizzes
Little David Learns to Earn a Lot of Money

Table of Contents

We would like to say thank you to our Local Parish, to all Charismatic Communities for sharing about our Faith Journey to our Lord Jesus Christ.

Thank you also to our Team and Family who working hard to get this book published.

HOW TO PRAY A GOOD PRAYER AND SIMPLE GUIDE FOR NORMAL PEOPLE AND GET ANSWERED (WITH TESTIMONIES)

The Blessed Creation

CHAPTER I
ARE YOU ACTUALLY PRAYING?

We all know how to say prayers, but some of us does not know how to pray. Everyone can say prayers, but that does not mean that they are actually praying.

Everyone is quite good as a Vocal Prayer, to become A Truly Prayer, minimum we need to have 4 things, which are:

1. Attention
2. Devotion
3. Faith
4. And Forego

We must be aware of what we are saying and should be saying it with love, faith and forego as well on the same time.

Jesus told us in Matthew 6:7, "Do not heap up empty phrases as the Gentiles do, for they think that they will be heard for their many words".

There are five types of prayer in the tradition of the Church, here are brief descriptions of each type of prayer, with examples of each.

1. **Worship and Adoration**

In prayers of Worship or Adoration, we honor the greatness of God, and we acknowledge our dependence on Him in all things.

Normally we find these in Mass and the other liturgies of the Church, which are full of prayers of adoration or worship, such as the Glory to God and/or Agnus Dei.

2. Intercession

It is praying for others, it is another form of petition, but they are important enough to be considered their own type of prayer.

In a prayer of intercession, we're not concerned with our needs but we concern for the needs of others, which leads us to pray as Jesus did.

Also we will find this in Abraham prayed for Sodom, even though he was not living in Sodom, we can read in Genesis 18 for more details.

3. Petition

Prayers of petition are the type of prayer which we are most familiar. Normally we ask God for things we need, physical and/or spiritual needs.

It is very important that our prayers of petition should be saying it with love, faith and forego; always include of our willingness to accept God's Will, whether our God answers exactly as our prayer or not.

4. Thanksgiving

Praying "Grace" before meals is a good example of The Thanksgiving prayer. It is better if we have habit of thanking God throughout the day for all the good things that happen to us and others as well.

Thanksgiving prayer is very good to build a better relation to our God.

5. Praise

We acknowledge God for what He is. We praise our God for his own sake and gives him glory, entirely beyond what he does, but simply because of HIM as HIMSELF. It shares in the blessed happiness of the pure of heart who love God in faith before seeing him in glory.

We find these prayer in The Psalms, or when we see a beautiful flowers as His Creation and we praise Him for His Creation.

One of the greatest ways to learn how to pray is to listen to great Prayers. In this case, we can learn from our Bible. Scripture is an excellent place to learn how to pray.

There are some inspired pages, we find eminent some Special Person who walked with God, and who held conversation with God in formal and informal settings in The Old Testament. Their prayers give us precious models of how we should pray.

We will read in this book about:

A. Prayer in our current modern world and the Testimony of each Prayer

(These are the actual testimonies in our current world, such as Covid-19 experiences and how Our Lord got involve, etc.)

B. Revealing more details about what Jesus told us for how to pray, you may not know these important points before (Chapter VIII, please read this).

C. We will learn how some of The Special Person in our Bible prayed to our Lord and the Testimony of each Prayer in Old Testament

D. And please read Chapter XVIII about The Conclusion, you may not know this very important conclusion about Praying before.

I believe that you ever have a hard conversation about Christianity in your communities, where you don't know how to respond wisely? Someone may asked you these:

> Are there still Answered Prayers Today?
> Are there still Any Miracles Today?

I know that it is not easy to answer these questions, and take time to explain these kind of questions. Then this person may push you with more questions as well.

> In our current world now, does God still perform miracles?
> Is there actually such thing as answered prayers?

So in the next chapters, we will read some Testimonies in "our Todays World ". The following chapters are happened in "our Todays World" about How to pray and The Answered Prayers. We will read the Testimonies in several occasion as well.

CHAPTER II
TESTIMONY FOR ANSWERED PRAYER ABOUT COVID 19

I have friends who got the Covid 19 last year. Their first signs of the disease began just four days before the Victoria Government of Australia locked people down for the Covid 19, he started feeling unwell.

He got sick and it was just like a normal flu and I thought it wasn't that serious," he told me.

He attempted to get tested at the clinic in Melbourne, Australia but was rejected because he didn't have a sore throat and wasn't coughing. The next three days, he got the testing.

His wife was also affected with the coronavirus. He told the doctor after taking his test whether his wife can got the test as well, and The Doctor said no," he recalled.

"The doctor said just wait to get his result first. "

They were sick and their son lives in Queensland, so only two of them in their house, so they were looking at each other and discussing and thinking for trying to avoid away the pain.

By the time he got the results, it confirmed that he had the coronavirus, his wife condition was much more serious than him.

She got a high fever, a very bad non-stop cough. She told my friend to take her straight to the hospital.

Due to so many patient in the hospital and the strict COVID-19 rules, the security would not allow him to enter into the hospital with his wife. They asked him to go home.

He told me that it was so sad for him and he worried because her wife went inside in the hospital by herself with her condition.

He did not went home, but stayed in the car park for about 60 minutes confused and worried. He didn't know what to do. But finally he prayed to Our Father to ask Our Father to look after his wife. After he prayed he just settled down because of his faith in Our Lord.

Her wife told me over the phone later that she walked into the hospital feeling weak and kept coughing. There was a Nurse asked her,

"What's going on?"

"What's happening?"

So she explained everything then she was unconscious according to the Nurse after she recovered. She was in ICU when she recovered.

The pair both have a strong Christian faith.

He kept telling me that during that time he stayed hopeful.

Later in late afternoon his wife called him, she said, that she was in ICU. She asked him to pray for her. That was the last time that he heard from her. He didn't say goodbye and that's the hardest thing about it.

He just dropped his wife in front of the hospital and said,

'I'll just park the car, then come and to see you'.

Not knowing that he could not enter the hospital. So he didn't know that was the last time to see her wife and he didn't even say goodbye to her wife.

It was hard for him.

My friend slowly but sure recovered from Covid-19, his symptoms had gone. He was left home alone, even though he has hope but he was worrying as well about his wife and not knowing when he would see her next.

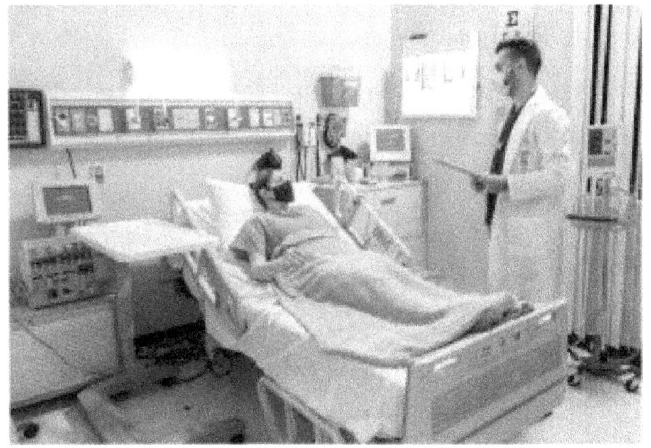

Her wife condition was serious and she was sedated for an entire month.

At one point doctors told the family they didn't expect her to survive. His wife was unable to breathe on her own.

During that time their son from Queensland has returned to Melbourne with special permission from The Health Authority of Victoria. Their son was still in quarantine, but their son started to pray-circle together. Their son gathered family members and friends around the world using Facebook, Instagram, Twitter, Pinterest to pray for her mother through daily Zoom, including myself from Sydney with Zoom as well.

One of the verse which we used many times during the Zoom Praying was from Philippians 4, verses 6-7:

[6] Never worry about anything; but tell God[1] all your desires of every kind in prayer[2] and petition shot through with gratitude,

[7] and the peace of God[3] which is beyond our understanding will[4] guard your hearts and your thoughts in Christ[5] Jesus.

A lot of people prayed, they stood together and it was amazing. People that don't know Jesus came together and prayed.

My friend told me that because of this Zoom Prayers helped his wife to recover step by step. Our Father answered our prayer.

After five weeks in ICU his wife was taken off the sedatives and began breathing on her own for the first time in weeks. My friend recalled his wife first words:

"It was just 'Praise God!'

His wife moved to the COVID-19 recovery ward and my friend was finally able to see his wife again. It was the first time since he dropped her at the hospital more than five weeks ago.

---

1.   https://www.catholic.org/encyclopedia/view.php?id=5217

2.   https://www.catholic.org/prayers

3.   https://www.catholic.org/encyclopedia/view.php?id=5217

4.   https://www.catholic.org/encyclopedia/view.php?id=12332

5.   https://www.catholic.org/clife/jesus

My friend told me that it was the longest time that they had ever been separated having been used to doing everything together.

Over the phone to me, both of them told me that the experience has strengthened their faith to Our Lord better than ever, as well as their marriage.

The couple are full of praise - for Our Lord and the Health Staff who look after his wife. They prayed for the Health Staff and asked Jesus to Bless them all and give them peace and joy and healthy as well during the difficult time, especially from the Health Staff around the world with this Pandemic Covid-19.

CHAPTER III

TESTIMONY FOR ANSWERED PRAYER ABOUT WEDDING DRESSES

I have another a family friend who asked me to pray for her daughter wedding dresses. She is okay if I write about her and her daughter story in this book for sharing her journey.

Her daughter told her that she would really love some new dresses for the different occasions during her wedding celebration and her wedding party. She would be wearing a wedding dress, and gown for part of the day but in different times she wouldn't be wearing a gown. Her daughter wished that she had a couple of new dresses for the events.

Her husband had been out of work because of the Pandemic Covid-19, and her salary was just enough to cover her monthly expenses. So she can't have any additional expenses that come with her daughter wedding party, including some new dresses.

She told me that she began to pray about the situation. She had been praying for a job for her husband. Now she was praying for dresses for her daughter as well.

She told me that it was very difficult for her to inform her daughter that she could not help her daughter to buy some new dresses. Or to tell her daughter that do not ask if her daughter need something to her. Her daughter was the only child she got. She wanted to make her daughter happy.

She told me that she kept on praying. And she told me that she would like to take a Casual Job in Saint Vincent de Paul Society Shop in Sydney to get a bit more money for buying dresses for her daughter.

I told her that was a great idea, so we kept praying and she did something as well on the same time by working more as a Casual Staff in Saint Vincent de Paul Society Shop.

Two weeks before her wedding party, Saint Vincent de Paul Society Shop in Sydney Australia, where she worked as Casual Staff received a big parcel of donated items from a non-profit organization that they had partnered with.

Within this donation were six brand new dresses as well. They were expensive dresses and beautiful. They were pretty, and how about the sizes? The sizes were her daughter size. She was really happy and she was sure that it was Jesus's hand who arranged this!

So she informed her Shop Manager about her situation. Her Manager told her that she could buy some with the Staff Price. If her daughter needed more than she could buy, her daughter could borrow them for her wedding and returned them back to the shop later, without pay anything for the borrowing dresses.

She immediately called her daughter and MMS her pictures of the dresses. Her daughter was so excited and her as well. When her daughter tried them on, they fit her perfectly!

The next day, she called me, she said:

"What an amazing answer to our prayers".

"What an opportunity to share this blessing with her daughter"

CHAPTER IV

TESTIMONY FOR ANSWERED PRAYER ABOUT MARRIAGE

One of my family friend was sharing to me about her marriage issues and asked me to pray for her. She told me that she is okay for me to write her journey in this book, to let our Readers to understand and maybe have something to learn.

According to her, she has a long journey of faith, patience, and learning to trust God's promises more than anything.

Most days, she cried because of her husband.

She thought a healthy marriage is not supposed to be this way. She remembered how wonderful her marriage had started. Everyday there were a lot of giggles and a lot of joy in her family.

Then after the death of her daughter, her husband changed totally. Her husband fell into deep depression, deep trauma, starting to have a kind of isolation to his soul and body. And seem to her that her husband hate her and blamed her for the death of her daughter as well.

She would like to have another children to cherish her husband and make him back as before again. But it almost impossible for them with their situation at that time.

She felt bitterness, alone, anger, abandoned and rejected as a wife and a woman. She was devastated and desperate. Her marriage was dying.

She started to seek God intensely and pour out her heart to Jesus, praying and she developed the daily habit to read and study the Bible.

Sadly her husband was not a believer like her. But she kept praying everyday asking Our Father to help her.

One day, she came to see me to inform her latest journey again. During that time, after she told me about the latest condition, I mentioned about Matthew 22 verse 39. Jesus told us to love our neighbour as we love ourselves. I made her remember how Jesus was able to forgive the Roman Soldiers and so on. Basically about forgiving to other person.

She became aware that she need to do a bit as well to make her marriage getting better. Not only asking to her husband had to change only. She promised to me for not just passive recipients of answered prayers without responsibility.

She realized that she had an important things to play as well. She realized that she made a mistake by asking her husband to change, because she could not make it happened.

The next morning she called me, she told me that she just realized that actually her husband helped her a lot about her housekeeping, make breakfast every day for her, etc. Which for some reason, she "could not see" and she could not appreciate them at all before. She told me that she saw "another person" in her husband. She started to appreciate him and realized that she need to help her husband to recover from his trauma of losing their daughter. Previously she just blamed him, without helping and understood him at all about his trauma.

She told me that she did not stop praying, trusting that God knows what He is doing to bring her marriage back to life.

She became more aware of the gradual change in her husband.

She told me that she prayed and asking Jesus turned her husband sorrows into repentance, bringing him to a new beginning and life with God. And she again asked me to pray for her and for her husband as well. Both for her marriage and for her husband faith to Jesus as well.

One day she called me to thank me for everything that I have done to her and her husband. She told me that her life and the changes in her in seeing and treating her husband were his living sermon and proof for God's love. She told me that she was his living manifestation of God's grace. I told her to praise to Jesus, not necessary to thanks to me. Jesus has done it together with her.

On her 11th anniversary of her wedding, she has earned back her marriage, and her husband was baptised, accepting by faith forgiveness and justification in Jesus Christ.

She told me to mention in this book to tell our Readers that God is Faithful and He Answers Our Prayers. Before she thought this would be the most impossible thing to happen. But she got it, so she would like to inform everyone about this Great News.

She told me to mention about The First Letter from Peter, 1 Peter 3, verses 1-4:

"In the same way, you wives must submit yourselves to your husbands, so that if any of them do not believe God's word, your conduct will win them over to believe. It will not be necessary for you to say a word. Because they will see how pure and reverent your conduct is. You should not use outwards aids to make yourselves beautiful, such as the way you do your hair, or jewellery you put on, or the dresses you wear. Instead, your beauty should consist of your true inner self, the ageless beauty of a gentle and quiet spirit, which is of the greatest value in God's sight"

CHAPTER V
TESTIMONY FOR ANSWERED PRAYER ABOUT JOB

I have another testimony to share about answered prayer, this time is about finding a Job. One of our congregation told me that he got his redundancy due to the current Pandemic Covid-19 around 3 months ago.

He was looking for a job and he asked me to pray for him. He is okay if I write about his journey in this book.

He complained, why Our Father did not answer his prayer for finding a job for him. He asked me, whether:

"Was Our Father hearing me?"

"Has He chosen to ignore me?"

"Did He not care?"

"Why He did for other believers but not to me?"

And of course there were a lot of others questions as well.

So we discussed with him about these issues based from what we learn from our Bible (Old Testament and New Testament as well).

I have established with him, that for sure Our Father hears our prayers. He doesn't ignore us. We read in 1 John 5, verse 14 says that the confidence we have in God is that if we ask anything according to His will, He hears us.

And I deeply discussed with him about this key phrase is

"If we ask according to His will."

This is very important thing, he promised me to check and try to listen Our Lord "voice" about His Will. Thus far, he was the only one who keep asking and talking and ignoring Our Father respond.

Another one which I established with him is

"Do Not Lose Your Heart".

He promised me to keep praying

We discuss about the other side to see the issue as well, for instance rather than ask,

"Why didn't Our Father answer my prayer for a job?" a better question would be,

"What is Our Father's answer to my prayer for a job?"

We were wondering that maybe Our Father has answered our prayers, but we don't recognize His answers because we are not paying attention to them. Because we just want to get The Instant Result and get exactly as we want it?

After several days meeting him discussing why he did not get his job, I can make summaries about our discussion as below:

1. Do we do a bit for finding this job?

He realized that previously he just wait upon Our Father to give him a job, but he did not do anything about it.

He promised me to do a lot things for finding his job, such as upload his CV in Job Seeker, Go to Centre Link, tell his friends, etc.

He promised me to actively see the Job Ad as daily basis and if he finds some, he will apply as well.

2. God's Will:

We need to ask:

"Is our prayer in line with God's will?"

"Is our prayer getting a job due to the perks it offers or the prestige which we will get for that job?"

I told him that he can pray and ask Our Lord to show him whether he was praying with the right job for him.

You may be praying for a job that is not in line with God's Will. Our Father may have a better job for us for long term, which was still temporary was not exist for a while. Maybe Our Father ask us to become His Hand to do other things? The one which was still waiting will be better for us, even though was not exist thus far.

Maybe God wants you to start your own business?

There is a possibility that Our Father will give us a completely different answer to our prayers. Can be better, exceeding our imaginations and desires.

3. The Appointed Time

He understood that everything need time. I told him that Our Father has to work things out in his favour, and this may take some time.

He will give you a job that requires a preparation time before you are ready for it. He wants to bless you with the very best as you patiently wait for Him.

4. The other side to consider

He agreed that our lives are unique, and the reasons why we don't get answers to our prayers for a job are varied. But Our Father can enlighten him regarding his situation and point him in the right direction. Sometimes, we are on the right track with our prayer, and we just need to be patient and wait for Our Father's timing.

When I am writing this book, he is still jobless due to the condition of this Pandemic, and the good news is he understood that Our Lord is working for him, together with his effort to find a suitable job for him.

During that time, The New South Wales Government in Australia gave him a Disaster Payment for a person like him. So he is okay for "his daily bread". He told me that he will not lose his heart and he will keep praying and try to seriously listen what Our Father want him to do.

CHAPTER VI

TESTIMONY FOR ANSWERED PRAYER ABOUT FINANCE DIFFICULTIES

I have a friend who is an Evangelist like me, he devoted his life 100 % to Our Father and having 100 % Faith to Our Father as well. His wife did the same as well.

He told me his story:

After his second year of marriage, his wife and himself felt the Lord leading them toward full-time evangelism, and linked up with a college ministry that sent couples on mission trips to a variety of campuses around Australia. He resigned from his permanent jobs and travelling around the country. He was surprised to learn that this well-intentioned, but not well organized ministry and almost without any financial support to him.

It was a shock to learn that he was pretty much on his own. But believing that Jesus had led them down to this path, my friend and his wife chose to continue on at least for 6 months.

They did not have any other options, they have to really 100 % relying only on God to provide for them, even for "the daily bread". Finally he reckoned that this was what God and The Ministry really had in mind all along. The Ministry did not give them enough money for the travelling cost, it was on purpose. The Ministry used this experience to teach all Evangelist how to trust Our Father to meet their needs.

He had personally never been through anything like this, so far from home, with little money or resources. Not even friends or family to turn to.

When they were in Northern Territory in Australia close to Alice Springs. My friend and his wife pressed forward, pulling a small camper behind their car. They prayed and stood on the promises of Jesus, that He never failed us.

They nearly ran out of money or provisions on many occasions, but somehow Jesus always met our need. Sometimes strangers just walked up and just handed us money, even in cities which my friend never visited before. Sometimes he was scheduled to do talk anywhere in Churches to share or preach, and the congregation gave them some free-will offerings that helped meet their need.

Sometimes they were in very trying moments, such as during their visit to Darwin. By the end of the month spent there, their money and resources were drained. They had less than 10 dollars, with a near empty gas tank. He and his wife returned to their little camper that night, he felt discouraged and ready to give up, but they knelt and prayed throughout the evening until both of them fell asleep.

The next thing he remember was awaking to a knocking at the trailer door. They did not any friend there, so he opened the door cautiously. There was a boy standing there with a big smile, holding several grocery bags. He said

"These are for you mate,"

Then that boy turned away.

Barely awake, my friend and his wife were shocked by this boy's brief visit. They looked through the sacks, we found groceries and other items, and they found some of their preferred brands which they like for their food. And in the bottom of one sack, was an envelope of cash, just enough to fill the gas tank to the next destination!

Nobody knew their need or how much they needed for the petrol, except Our Lord. Before doing anything else that morning, they spent time thanking and praising Our Lord for hearing their prayers, and for meeting their needs again, as He did last time and again and again!

That was my friend testimony that Our Lord was looking after him and his wife, including money and or his "daily bread".

Many Christians are struggling financially due to unforeseen circumstances. With the economy in the state that it is in, they cannot seem to find a job that pays them enough to cover their bills. They try everything they can, but nothing seems to work.

One of the most common prayers is

"God, help me make enough money so I can pay my bills and provide for my family".

Answered prayer for money has been a practice of praying for things that were not possible without prayer. Our Father has already made the provision and people's prayer are supposed to be in line with what he has already done.

CHAPTER VII

TESTIMONY FOR ANSWERED PRAYER ABOUT NATION

I would like to make you remember about this story of MIRACLES OF DUNKIRK, written By Evan Miller from Mysterious Ways posted in God's Grace, Nov. 14, 2017, Guideposts (permitted to be shared as in Mysterious Ways Magazine)

I believe that most of us still remember about this story or heard about this real story in modern world. You may have seen the hit movie Dunkirk, director Christopher Nolan's powerful tribute to the real-life World War II drama that unfolded over 10 days in 1940, on the shores of France.

For Winston Churchill, the new British prime minister, it all began with an early phone call on May 15.

"We have been defeated," said the French premier, Paul Reynaud.

"We are beaten."

Churchill was aware of the Nazi advance. Days earlier, Adolf Hitler's army had taken Holland, Belgium and Luxembourg, with Denmark and Norway already in his grip. England had sent more than 200,000 troops to France and Belgium.

"Surely it can't have happened so soon?" the stunned Churchill said.

"The front is broken," Reynaud said. "The Nazis are pouring through in great numbers."

The Allies had severely miscalculated the path the Nazis would take. The Germans had swept south, through the supposedly impenetrable Ardennes Forest, a region the Allies had barely bothered to defend. Now British and French troops found themselves surrounded, in disarray. Their only possible escape was across the English Channel. Through Dunkirk, a city in northeast France. A mass evacuation would require funnelling thousands upon thousands of soldiers, spread across hundreds of miles, into one space while the Nazis closed in with 1,800 tanks and 300 Stuka dive-bombers.

Churchill resisted that escape plan. It seemed like a suicide mission. They'd be lucky to get 20,000 men home via the English Channel, let alone more than 300,000 Allied troops. But there was no other option.

On May 23, Churchill met with the British monarch, King George VI, to brief him. Though a naval rescue operation were under way, pitifully few ships were ready to sail. The logistics of defending against the inevitable German air attack while ferrying the troops seemed impossible. Allied soldiers were scrambling to reach Dunkirk. They barely knew which direction to go.

"We must pray," King George VI said. "This next Sunday, I'm calling for a national day of prayer."

Churchill was surely not looking at prayer as the answer. But he could hardly refuse the king.

On May 24, King George VI addressed the nation: **"Let us with one heart and soul, humbly but confidently, commit our cause to God and ask His aid, that we may valiantly defend the right as it is given to us to see it."**

On May 26, at Westminster Abbey, the Archbishop of Canterbury called on God to protect the troops. Across Great Britain, tens of thousands of people responded to the king's call, uniting as never before. Cathedrals and churches, mosques and synagogues were packed to overflowing. At Westminster Cathedral, the line extended for blocks and hundreds kept vigil outside. The people didn't know exactly why they were praying, yet they prayed even so.

"Nothing like this has ever happened before" was how one English newspaper described the scene.

The following day, though, the German High Command reported, "The British army is encircled, and our troops are proceeding to its annihilation." The war, it appeared, was over for the Allies. Few would have argued otherwise.

The soldiers were instructed to "get back to Dunkirk." Where? Most British soldiers had probably never even heard of Dunkirk.

Everywhere, the roads were filled with British and French soldiers. Abandoned tanks and equipment littered the countryside. Thousands of refugees marched with escaping troops, some driving cars, everyone fleeing in advance of the Germans. From out of the skies would come the Stukas, strafing everything in sight. The scene was horrific.

But all was not as it appeared.

Something happened that historians, even 77 years later, can't explain. With German tanks rumbling just 10 miles from Dunkirk, Hitler did the unthinkable. On May 24, the day King George VI called the nation to pray, Hitler inexplicably halted the offensive. For nearly three days, as England knelt as one, those tanks remained grounded. Nothing moved.

It was the exact window of time the British needed to form a defensive perimeter, to temporarily fight back the Germans and establish a funnel for their troops to flow through to the English Channel.

Then came something else. Rain and clouds. German planes bombed Dunkirk on three separate days, but each time, for days afterward, the city was enveloped by inclement weather, making any effective follow-up from the Nazis difficult. What's more, a breeze seemed to collect smoke emitted from the German bombs and distribute it over the area the British were using to load men into boats. The Allied exodus went undetected for days.

Meanwhile, word was spreading across England of the need for boats to cross the channel to Dunkirk. For what purpose no one was exactly sure. Almost any vessel would do. Rowboats. Fishing trawlers. Tugs. Motorboats. Hundreds of would be skippers responded. Some had never been out of sight of land before. Many of the crafts lacked compasses. None of them were armed.

Robert Hilton, a physical education instructor, and Ted Shaw, a cinema manager, were among those who answered the call. They joined a makeshift crew with a motorboat, Rye gate II. But when they reached the town of Ramsgate, off the tip of southern England, the only supplies they were given were two cans of water. Not even a cup to drink with. The two of them went to a pub, downed a pint, pocketed the glasses and set off toward France.

The English Channel is notoriously rough, choppy—no place for novice seamen—but once again something peculiar happened. The water Hilton and Shaw encountered was like that of a bathtub, with barely a ripple to disturb the journey. No one had ever seen anything like it. There were so many boats that in places the waters resembled a freeway at rush hour.

James Bradley, the machine gunner, eventually reached De Panne, Belgium, just east of Dunkirk. Over the sand hills, he could see thousands of soldiers huddled, a line of small boats coming in to the shore and ferrying the men to larger vessels in the deeper water, guarded over by ships with guns. They'll never get these people off here, he thought.

But it was happening. From De Panne and Dunkirk. A few boats at a time, offloading a few dozen men, then coming back for more, round the clock, a dizzying spectacle.

The Rye gate II limped into the waters off France, her engines broken, her propeller twisted by wreckage. Robert Hilton and Ted Shaw tied up to a larger boat and manned one of its lifeboats. For 17 hours straight, they rowed soldiers from shore to ship.

In the first five days of the rescue mission, more than 100,000 soldiers were evacuated. That still left more than 200,000 men, tens of thousands desperately fighting to hold the perimeter. They'd be the last to go.

Bradley never forgot the hero's welcome he received when he at last reached the shores of England. The tables loaded with tea and buns. The crowds of people waving, cheering. This is England, he thought. You're worth fighting for. Hilton and Shaw would also remember the cheers that greeted them. Exhausted, they and the other crew members somehow managed to get the crippled Rye gate II back to England, throngs of jubilant well-wishers at every bridge on the Thames River.

By then, 338,000 soldiers had made it safely across the English Channel as well, thanks to the efforts of about 850 "little ships." There was a feeling of determination, not surrender. Deliverance by a divine hand. It was exactly what the British soldiers—and civilians—needed to forge ahead. Especially so early in the war.

On June 4, Churchill went to the House of Commons to deliver the news. "We shall fight on the beaches," he thundered. "We shall fight on the landing grounds, we shall fight in the fields and in the streets."

***The Prime Minister called it a miracle, a word he was not known to often use. There seemed no other word to describe it.* Not just one, but a whole series of miracles. Without any one of them, the entire operation would have failed. Hitler halting the blitzkrieg. The thick, protective cloud cover. The English Channel growing still. The hundreds of tiny boats, appearing seemingly from out of nowhere.**

Despite many ships being sunk and many lives lost, by the end of the operation on 4 June, Ramsay, his ships and staff had rescued 338,226 British and Allied troops landed them in England. The rescue came to be regarded as a 'miracle', and remains the largest amphibious evacuation undertaken in wartime.

CHAPTER VIII

TESTIMONY FROM OUR LORD JESUS CHRIST ABOUT HOW TO PRAY

As we read in our Bible, the disciples were with Jesus most of the time and they were with Him when He went to pray and heard his prayers to God. But they still weren't sure how they were supposed to do it. So Jesus told them, how to pray. Jesus Christ said to the disciples that we should keep our prayers simple. Our Father listens to us no matter if our prayers are long or short. Even if we don't have the right words, Our Father knows what we mean without having to use delicate words.

Jesus also said that we shouldn't show off when we pray.

Jesus said this especially to the people that used to stand on the street corners praying, so that everyone would think how great they were at praying.

He wants us to pray in a quiet place with our own words.

We need to tell Our Father about our needs,

Give Him thanks,

Praise Him,

And tell Him what we're sorry for.

Now, we will learn from The Lord Himself.

We will carefully learn word by word to get more deeply understanding and truly practicing as well as a daily basis in "Our Father" or also known as "The Lord's Prayer".

The question of,

"How do we pray?"

It is the one which is often asked and one that was posed thousands of years ago by the disciples.

We can read in Mathew 6: 9-13 or in Luke 11:1-4, when one of Jesus' disciples ask Him,

"Lord, teach us to pray,"

Jesus replied by giving us the prayer that we recite countless times throughout our lifetime. It is

The Our Father or Pater Noster

Also known as

The Lord's Prayer

What is the Lord's Prayer?

Jesus instructed His disciples and us to:

"Pray, then, in this way", in Luke 11, verses 1-4

Now it happened that he was in a certain place praying, and when he had finished, one of his disciples said, 'Lord, teach us to pray, as John[1] taught his disciples.'

[2] He said to them, 'when you pray, this is what to say: Our Father, may your name be held holy, your kingdom come;

[3] give us each day our daily bread, and forgive us our sins,

[4] for we ourselves forgive each one who is in debt[2] to us. And do not put us to the test.'

Actually this is a short prayer, it will take around 20 seconds to say, but it is filled with incredible meaning.

It is The Best Prayer which perfectly summarized of what Christians believe, how Christian should live and what's expressed in the Gospels, the Lord Prayer is it.

---

1.   *https://www.catholic.org/bible/book.php?id=50*

2.   *https://www.catholic.org/encyclopedia/view.php?id=3701*

There are some great devotion, huge praise to our Lord, some spiritual strength and contains all of our prayers and petitions as well in this short prayer. It is really awesome and spectacular.

We have been a practicing Christian since we were little, so I believe that we have been reciting this prayer more times than you can count.

As other thing we do repeatedly, saying this prayer silently or out loud becomes second nature.

Due to this condition, it is very important for us to remind ourselves to slow down and to reflect on the words by words for what we are saying. Let's learn at what each line means, and how we can apply this prayer to our lives in a daily basis.

Reflecting on the Meaning of the Lord's Prayer:

1. Our Father, Who art in heaven

a. First thing first, the first word of this prayer, it is OUR:

We noticed that Jesus did not instruct us to say "**MY** FATHER", but on the other hand Jesus stressed on "**OUR** FATHER". So Jesus Christ did not want us to keep Our Father for myself or for yourselves ONLY.

Jesus Christ did not want us to be selfish and keep Our Father to individual only.

We have another deeply important in this word of OUR. With this word of OUR, Jesus asked us to have mercy to other people as well. So Jesus asked us to treat other people as OUR Family members as well.

Can we do it? Normally we can do it for someone who not having any issues with us.

But can we treat someone who has a problem with us?

Someone who hate us?

Someone who make us hurt very much?

This opening address also unites Christians worldwide into one community of worshippers as we pray to "our" Father and not individually to "my" Father.

This reminds us that we recognize all those around us as children of God and treat them with mercy accordingly as well.

b. Now we are thinking about the second word of this prayer, which is "Father":

We must remember that none of the saints had in Scripture never address God as their Father. The invocation places us at once in the centre of the wonderful revelation the Son came to make of His Father as our Father too.

It embraces the mystery of redemption, Jesus Christ delivering us from the curse that we might become the children of God. Through Jesus Christ, The Son of God, the Spirit in the new birth giving us the new life, so we have OUR FATHER.

And the mystery of our faith, before the redemption is accomplished, the word is given to the disciples to prepare them for the blessed experience still to come. This words are the key to the whole prayer, to all prayer. It means so deeply and a game changer for human being in the world.

Even though the knowledge of God's Father-love is a simplest enough, but also the last and highest lesson in the school of prayer.

It is in the personal relation to the living God, and the personal conscious fellowship of love with Himself, that prayer begins. It is in the knowledge of God's Fatherliness, revealed by the Holy Spirit, that the power of prayer will be found to root and grow also making "fruit" as well.

In the infinite tenderness and pity and patience of the infinite Father, in His loving readiness to hear and to help, the life of prayer has its joy.

Let us take time, until the Spirit has made these words to us spirit and truth, filling heart and life: 'Our Father who art in heaven.' Then we are indeed within the veil, in the secret place of power where prayer always prevails.

c. Then for "*who art in Heaven*"

Then we are professing our core religious belief that God is our heavenly Father, the one who is all knowing and all powerful. "Our

Father who art in heaven" means we're praying to our Heavenly Father who lives in heaven.

God likes it when we call Him Father, and He wants us to talk to Him just like we talk to our own father. God is our loving Father, and we are His special children.

This address reaffirms our core belief as Christians that God is our celestial Father, both with us in spirit and above us in the perfect realm of Heaven.

2. Hallowed be Thy Name

Hallowed means holy. God's name is holy, as God is the paragon of sanctity. "There is no one holy like the Lord", we can read in 1 Samuel 2:2[3].

Even though God wants us to call him Our Father, he is still God, and He is to be respected and honoured.

There is something here that strikes us at once. While we ordinarily first bring our own needs to God in prayer, and then think of what belongs to God and His interests, the Master reverses the order.

The lesson is of more importance than we think. In true worship the Father must be first, must be all. The sooner I learn to forget myself in the desire that HE may be glorified, the richer will the blessing be that prayer will bring to myself.

No one ever loses by what he sacrifices for the Father.

This must influence to all our prayer. There are two sorts of prayer: personal and intercessory. The latter ordinarily occupies the lesser part of our time and energy. This may not be.

Jesus Christ has opened the school of prayer specially to train intercessors for the great work of bringing down, by their faith and prayer, the blessings of His work and love on the world around.

There can be no deep growth in prayer unless this be made our aim. The little child may ask of the father only what it needs for itself; and yet it soon learns to say, please give some for sister too.

---

3.   http://www.christianity.com/bible/search/?ver=niv&q=1+samuel+2:2

Another thing to think of "Hallowed be Thy name". What name? This new name of Father. The word of Holy is the central word of the Old Testament; so the "Name of Father" is the New Name. In this name of Love all the holiness and glory of God are now to be revealed. And how is the name to be hallowed?

By God Himself would reveal the holiness, the Divine power, the hidden glory of the name of Father. The Spirit of the Father is the Holy Spirit: it is only when we yield ourselves to be led of Him, that the name will be hallowed in our prayer and our lives. As we pray: Our Father, hallowed be Thy name.'

As Christians, we understand that the Almighty Father is to be revered and praised above all else. In this petition, we pray that the entire world will recognize the holy name of God as the one true God of all, the Creator and Ruler of the universe.

Hallowed is another word for holy or sanctified. When we say "hallowed be Thy name," we are not only telling God "I recognize that you are holy".

But more importantly, we're asking that His name be recognized by everyone throughout the world as being the ultimate holy power—that one day (sooner rather than later) all will know Him to be righteous, powerful, and everyone's one true God and one ONLY.

3. Thy Kingdom come, Thy will be done on earth as it is in Heaven

There are several explanation of this word of prayer.

This petition has a two-fold meaning.

a. For "Thy Kingdom come":

If we think about where God lives, we know it is very great. The Bible told us that in heaven there will be no more crying, God live with us. There will be no hunger or bad things there.

So in this first part of prayer, we are praying that The Kingdom of God to take form in our world here and now.

b. For the other words of "Thy will be done, as in heaven, so on earth":

So that we can live in our world characterized by only goodness, honesty, faith, hope, and love one another, will be happened in our daily life.

So we are praying that we would live in peace and love one another, as the way it is in heaven. We can read more details in Mathew 22, verses 37-40 as well.

The other meaning of a "new heaven and a new earth" be fulfilled. When that promise is fulfilled, the faithful will live with God in His Kingdom eternally as members of a Holy City in which there is no death, crying, or pain.

We can read more details in Revelation 21, verse 1-4[4].

4. Give us this day our daily bread

We ask to Our Father to provide this for us, because we love and trust HIM. We are recognizing that every things we need come to us from Our Father. We ask Our Father give us today all that we really need.

Meaning all things that we can't live without. Those are the things that we want; we need food, water and shelter. Just as good food nourishes the body, the Good News nourishes the soul.

The Bible told us that "man shall not live on bread alone but on every word that comes from the mouth of God", please read in Deuteronomy 8, verse 3[5].

Give us this day our daily bread.' When first the child has yielded himself to the Father in the care for His Name, His Kingdom, and His Will.

He has full liberty to ask for his daily bread. A master cares for the food of his servant, a general of his soldiers, a father of his child.

And will not the Father in heaven care for the child who has in prayer given himself up to His interests?

4.	http://www.christianity.com/bible/search/?ver=niv&q=revelations+21%3a1-4

5.	http://www.christianity.com/bible/search/?ver=niv&q=deuteronomy+8:3

In this appeal, we also pray for the spiritual sustenance as well. Meaning that we can have to go out into the world and spread His Message through our words and our actions.

This nourishment comes from the Word of God and from communion with Christ, who is the "bread of life" that comes down from Heaven so that "whoever feeds on this bread will live forever". We can read more details in John 6, verses 48-58[6].

5. And forgive us our trespasses, as we forgive those who trespass against us

This is the toughest to pray and follow. But this request contains a great wisdom for long term period of time. Everybody can ask to receive forgiveness, if we combine with forgiving others as well, this can lead us to patience and distinguish than can be transformative. Jesus Christ his infinite wisdom teaches us that in order for Him to forgive our wrongdoings, we must first forgive those who've hurt us.

Jesus Christ is not being difficult, rather Jesus is teaching us that when there is bitterness and anger in our hearts, there's no room for His love to fill our hearts.

How can we ask God to be merciful and forgive our sins, if we're holding a grudge or refuse to forgive someone who's wronged us? This is a great wisdom.

As bread is the first need of the body, so forgiveness for the soul. And the provision for the one is as sure as for the other.

We are children, but sinners too; our right of access to the Father's presence we owe to the precious blood and the forgiveness it has won for us.

Let us beware of the prayer for forgiveness becoming a formality: only what is really confessed is really forgiven.

Let us in faith accept the forgiveness as promised: as a spiritual reality, an actual transaction between God and us, it is the entrance into all the Father's love and all the privileges of children.

---

6.   http://www.christianity.com/bible/search/?ver=niv&q=john+6%3a48-58

Such forgiveness, as a living experience, is impossible without a forgiving spirit to others: as forgiven expresses the heavenward, so forgiving the earthward, relation of God's child. In each prayer to the Father I must be able to say that I know of no one whom I do not heartily love.

By choosing to replace resentment with forgiveness, we reflect God's love and mercy in our actions. Then we will be able to walk more confidently toward God.

Forgiving someone is often easier said than done. Only God can give us the strength to do it through our prayer to Our Father.

6. And lead us not into temptation,

It is sometimes very tempting to do something you're not supposed to. This part is really neat because it asks Our Father to help us to know the right thing to do, to protect us against the evil that is in the world, and keep us away from it.

Temptation can cause us to sin and lead us away from God in ways that can be cumulative. God doesn't lead us to sin; we do that all on our own because of the free will our Creator gave us.

But our God is faithful and promises to provide a way out of any temptation that we may face.

Our daily bread, the pardon of our sins, and then our being kept from all sin and the power of the evil one, in these three petitions all our personal need is comprehended.

The prayer for bread and pardon must be accompanied by the surrender to live in all

Things, in holy obedience to the Father's will, and the believing prayer in everything to be kept by the power of the indwelling Spirit from the power of the evil one.

Jesus would have us to pray to the Father in heaven. To His Name, and Kingdom, and Will, have the first place in our love; His providing, and pardoning, and keeping love will be our sure portion.

So the prayer will lead us up to the true child-life: the Father all to the child. We shall understand how Father and child, the "Thine and the Our ", are all one, and how the heart that begins its prayer with the God-devoted THINE, will have the power in faith to speak out the OUR too.

Such prayer will, indeed, be the fellowship and interchange of love. In this supplication, we acknowledge that our free will brings with it human weaknesses. To overcome those weaknesses, we pray here for Our Father to extend His guiding hand over us and grant us the discernment necessary to steer clear of temptation and sin.

Temptation and sin go hand in hand. When we come face to face with temptation, it can sometimes be difficult to resist. That's why we need Our Father to set up the road blocks and lead us far away from the path of temptation.

7. But deliver us from evil.

Evil is an unfortunate reality in our world. The devil is always trying to tempt us and makes it his full-time job to look for ways to steer us from the right path and onto the wrong one.

The devil has no power over Our Father and when we pray to Our Father for protection against all that is evil, Our Father will shield us!

This petition covers the many times that we do fall prey to temptation and sin. During these times of complication if we continually seek to Our Father. Our Father will answer us and deliver us from all of our fears

In this appeal, we ask, during those times when we're mired in sin, that Our Father will reach us and liberate us from evil's grip. This petition is also one for protection, as we ask Our Father to protect us from the devil's grasp in all future circumstances.

We can learn from The Lord's Prayer:

1. If we think very deeply, we will think that The Lord's Prayer is actually reflects to Jesus life HIMSELF. Even in Mathew 6 verse 13, Jesus said, "Say this, how you should pray ". Jesus did not inform the disciples the options of prayers. Jesus just said:

"Say this ", that's it.

Jesus gave one prayer only. The way Jesus did, the way Jesus taught to the people and His Disciples.

The way Jesus depended on Our Father for His Material needs, the way Jesus encountered temptation and also the way Jesus forgave others. In other words, Jesus best known lesson on prayer is a lesson in praying out of one's own life experience.

2. There are many moving prayers that we can say, but when it comes to one prayer that takes the main aspects of our faith and summarizes them in several short lines, the Our Father is the perfect prayer.

3. Anyone can read the Lord's Prayer, but it's important to think about what you're saying. When you pray "give us this day your daily bread," think about all the things you have to be thankful for.

And how Our Father has given you everything you need, or things you need to ask for or pray for others. When you pray "forgive us our trespasses," ask forgiveness for those things you did wrong.

4. Prayer is our special way of talking to God, so remember to pray as many times as you can. God loves you and wants to know everything about you and how you're doing every day.

5. The Lord's Prayer is much more than a handy guide on what to pray when no other words come to mind. The prayer, if we meditate on each petition, serves as a moral compass that reveals the best way to go before the Father in requesting His guidance and protection.

6. The Lord's Prayer focuses our thoughts on what's important in life by summarizing all that we must do to be "good and faithful servants," namely: revere God, accept His will, know His Word, love each other through forgiveness, and resist evil.

7. Now it is a good time to say the Lord's Prayer together:

Our Father,
Who art in Heaven,
Hallowed be Thy Name.
Thy Kingdom come,
Thy will be done on earth
As it is in Heaven.
Give us this day our daily bread,
And forgive us our trespasses,
As we forgive those who trespass against us,
And lead us not into temptation,
But deliver us from evil.
Amen

As we all know in The Old Testament, there are some inspired pages, we find eminent some Special Person who walked with God, and who held conversation with God in formal and informal settings. Their prayers give us precious models of how we should pray, so let we discuss some of them in the next chapter.

CHAPTER IX
TESTIMONY FROM ABRAHAM

First we learn from Abraham. In the book of Genesis we read how Abraham is a fascinating person. He was a man of persistence, he never let his prayer life be superficial and he always took it to above the bar. In some ways, he negotiated and pushed God to the limit in his prayers.

Sometimes he got exactly for what he wanted. Sometimes he did not get what he wanted. Whatever the outcome of his prayers, but he continued to turn to the Lord in prayer. Abraham's prayers had a character and were specific and intentional.

Why not we learn from Abraham how to pray? Of course we can pray like Abraham. The Old Testament, there are some examples of who Abraham prayed for and how he prayed.

Genesis 20: 1-18

¹ Abraham left there for the region of the Negeb, and settled between Kadesh and Shur. While staying in Gerar,

² Abraham said of his wife Sarah, 'She is my sister,' and Abimelech the king of Gerar had Sarah brought to him.

3 *But God visited Abimelech in a dream one night. 'You are to die,' he told him, 'because of the woman you have taken, for she is a married woman.'*

4 *Abimelech, however, had not gone near her; so he said, 'Lord, would you kill someone even if he is upright?*

5 *Did he not tell me himself, "She is my sister"? And she herself said, "He is my brother." I did this with a clear conscience and clean hands.'*

6 *'Yes, I know,' God replied in the dream, 'that you did this with a clear conscience and I myself prevented you from sinning against me. That was why I did not let you touch her.*

7 *Now send the man's wife back; for he is a prophet and can intercede on your behalf for your life. But understand that if you do not send her back, this means death for you and all yours.'*

8 *Early next morning, Abimelech summoned his full court and told them the whole story, at which the people were very much afraid.*

9 *Then summoning Abraham, Abimelech said to him, 'What have you done to us? What wrong have I done you, for you to bring such guilt on me and on my kingdom? You had no right to treat me like this.'*

10 *Abimelech then said to Abraham, 'What possessed you to do such a thing?'*

11 *'Because', Abraham replied, 'I thought there would be no fear of God here and that I should be killed for the sake of my wife.*

12 *Anyway, she really is my sister, my father's daughter though not my mother's, besides being my wife.*

13 *So when God made me wander far from my father's home I said to her, "There is an act of love you can do me: everywhere we go, say of me that I am your brother."'*

14 *Abimelech took sheep, cattle, men and women slaves, and presented them to Abraham, and gave him back his wife Sarah.*

¹⁵ And Abimelech said, 'Look, my land is open to you. Settle wherever you please.'

¹⁶ To Sarah he said, 'Look, I am giving your brother a thousand pieces of silver. This will allay suspicions about you, as far as all the people round you are concerned; you have been completely vindicated.'

¹⁷ Abraham then interceded with God, and God healed Abimelech, his wife and his slave-girls, so that they could have children,

¹⁸ for Yahweh had made all the women of Abimelech's household barren on account of Sarah, Abraham's wife.

***A**braham prayed for those with whom he does not agree*: As we read as above on Genesis 20 we see where Abraham lies and convinces his wife to lie about who she is because he is fearful. Abimelech becomes angry when God reveals the truth, and confronts Abraham.

But with this condition, Abraham was still okay to pray for Abimelech and God heals Abimelech due to Abraham's intercession and even grants the ability for Abimelech's wife and maidservants to have children.

So we learn in this prayer that Abraham did not allow his relationship, or lack thereof, with Abimelech to prevent him from praying for Abimelech.

Normally we all have those people who have hurt us, we disagree with or maybe even those that scare us. We have people in our lives we dislike and those who are perhaps bitter enemies of ours. But why not we pray for them as Abraham prayed for Abimelech as we learn from his prayer.

Praying for those who have hurt us or have become some kind of enemy of ours is difficult. It may not be something we want to do. It is not meant to be easy but even Jesus prayed for those who were killing him on the cross.

We can read in Luke 23:34, "Then Jesus said, 'Father, forgive them, they know not what they do."

Another prayer from Abraham, which is very interesting:
Genesis 18: 20-33

20 Then Yahweh said, 'The outcry against Sodom and Gomorrah is so great and their sin is so grave,

21 that I shall go down and see whether or not their actions are at all as the outcry reaching me would suggest. Then I shall know.'

22 While the men left there and went to Sodom, Yahweh remained in Abraham's presence.

23 Abraham stepped forward and said, 'Will you really destroy the upright with the guilty?

24 Suppose there are fifty upright people in the city. Will you really destroy it? **Will you not spare the place for the sake of the fifty upright in it?**

25 Do not think of doing such a thing: to put the upright to death with the guilty, so that upright and guilty fare alike! Is the judge of the whole world not to act justly?'

26 Yahweh replied, 'If I find fifty upright people in the city of Sodom, I will spare the whole place because of them.'

27 Abraham spoke up and said, 'It is presumptuous of me to speak to the Lord, I who am dust and ashes:

²⁸ ***Suppose the fifty upright were five short?*** *Would you destroy the whole city because of five?' 'No,' he replied, 'I shall not destroy it if I find forty-five there.'*

²⁹ Abraham persisted and said, ***'Suppose there are forty to be found there?'*** *'I shall not do it,' he replied, 'for the sake of the forty.'*

³⁰ Abraham said, 'I hope the Lord will not be angry if I go on: Suppose there are only thirty to be found there?' 'I shall not do it,' he replied, 'if I find thirty there.'

³¹ He said, 'It is presumptuous of me to speak to the Lord: Suppose there are only twenty there?' 'I shall not destroy it,' he replied, 'for the sake of the twenty.'

³² He said, 'I trust my Lord will not be angry if I speak once more: ***perhaps there will only be ten.' 'I shall not destroy it,' he replied, 'for the sake of the ten.'***

³³ When he had finished talking to Abraham, Yahweh went away and Abraham returned home.

Abraham prays for a whole nation and negotiate with God:
As we know Abraham did not restrict his prayers to those of his inner circle. Abraham was not living in Sodom, bur he becomes a powerful intercessor for the judgment God eventually pours forth upon it. Abraham bargained with God. He begins by asking God

"What about those who innocent?"

"Will you sweep away the innocent with the guilty?"

"Suppose there were fifty innocent people within it?"

"Far be it from you to do such a thing, to make the innocent die with the guilty, so that the innocent and the guilty would be treated alike!"

"Should not the judge of all the world act with justice?"

As we can read on Genesis 18 as above, The Lord replied,

"If I find fifty innocent people in the city of Sodom, I will spare the whole place for their sake" (Genesis 18:23-26)

Then Abraham realizes how sinful Sodom is and reconsiders his request. He does not settle for God finding 50 innocent people, he even goes back to God in prayer and intercedes again. He asks God if he would spare Sodom if there were 45 innocent people found and God agrees.

This bargaining back and forth in prayer goes on until Abraham asks the Lord to spare Sodom if only 10 people were found in Sodom to be innocent. And the result was that The Lord agrees.

CHAPTER X
TESTIMONY FROM MOSES

Exodus 33:12-19

12 Moses said to Yahweh, 'Look, you say to me, "Make the people move on," but you have not told me whom you are going to send with me, although you have said, "I know you by name and you enjoy my favour."

13 If indeed I enjoy your favour, please show me your ways, so that I understand you and continue to enjoy your favour; consider too that this nation is your people.'

14 Yahweh then said, 'I myself shall go with you and I shall give you rest.'

15 To which he said, 'If you do not come yourself, do not make us move on from here,

16 for how can it be known that I and my people enjoy your favour, if not by your coming with us? By this we shall be marked out, I and your people, from all the peoples on the face of the earth.'

*17 Yahweh then said to Moses, '**Again I shall do what you have asked, because you enjoy my favour and because I know you by name.'***

18 He then said, 'Please show me your glory.'

19 Yahweh said, 'I shall make all my goodness pass before you, and before you I shall pronounce the name Yahweh; and I am gracious to those to whom I am gracious and I take pity on those on whom I take pity.

There are several aspect which we can read in Exodus 33 as above. Moses has just been informed that God would send Israel to Canaan with the promise of safe passage, with the Lord's angel going before them ONLY, but WITHOUT GOD come together with them as we can read in Exodus 33:1-3.

Israel was overwhelmed with grief by this news in Exodus 33:4-6. God's dwelling in their midst was what made them distinct, and now God was pulling back.

This separation is confirmed in 33:7-11, when Moses describes the kind of distant access Israel would be subjected to, now that the tabernacle plans had been destroyed in Exodus 32:19.

With the prospect of losing God's presence, Moses pleads for God's presence. Far more than the obligatory petition, **Moses gathered together all the promises God has made in the past, to make God changed His Mind**, so He is okay to re-join their caravan.

He pleads for God's presence, and he shows us how we ought to pray in the process. Please see several aspects:

1. Moses prays for God's presence:

Moses sees the immediate need and he prays for the return of God's presence. Moses prays for God (really nothing else), just GOD ONLY and ONLY GOD.

If God is going to do anything good in our lives, it is going to be underwritten by this sort of prayer–a very keen of desire for more of God. This is the heart behind Moses prayer, his passion for God's presence.

2. The goal of his prayer is knowledge:

In Exodus 33: 13, Moses prays that God would show His acts to Moses. Moses prayer rebukes anyone who has ever said about God or His word, "I know about that…" This kind of response reveals a heart that is self-reliant and reconfirm that we need having Christ in our life.

Unwillingness to learn about God is a personal invitation to destroy our professed faith.

Moses is a man unlike any other. If anyone knew God, it was Moses. Yet, his prayer reveals a desire to know God more. His model of prayer shows us that those who truly know God, long to know more of God.

Indeed, prayer that is Christian always presses to know God more and calls God to reveal himself more fully to those for whom we pray.

3. Favour comes through knowledge of the Lord:

The key to receiving God's favour and blessing is knowledge of God. Notice the progression in Exodus 33:13:

"If I have found favour in your sight"

It show the way Moses prays from grace unto grace.

"Please show me now your ways," marks the heart of the petition.

He desires to see and know God's ways,

"That I may know you."

The "that" signifies a purpose statement of knowing God, but that purpose statement is followed by another, deeper purpose statement, namely

"In order to find favour in our sight."

This is what Moses prayed for, and verses Exodus 14-15 confirm, that God heard his prayer, and answered him in the affirmative.

God graciously returned to the people of Israel. In the short term, Moses prayer effectively saved Israel

4. He prays according to God's promises:

Before his petitions, Moses reminds God of the "favour" God has already given him, and then prays based on this stated promise. This is a model for powerful prayer.

He prays from God's grace unto God's grace. **He requests favour, not based on his merits or his own spiritual ideas, but upon God's earlier favour.**

Thus, his prayer is according to God's will, not his own.

In our case, we can pray in Jesus Christ name. We are praying for favour based on God's love for the Son. Because of Christ's high priestly session, we are praying.

Therefore, we can pray those promises back to God in all are hours of need, and know that the Father will answer them with the rich supply that Christ obtained to the Cross for us.

5. Moses prayed with love, faith and forego as well on the same time:

Moses prayed with fully attention, love to our God with pure faith that God will give the people of Israel the best as has happened before.

And Moses has foregone everything to God to let God to make His Decision.

Accordingly, when we find ourselves distant from God, may we turn to him to find grace and our favour as well. As we come to know him, to pursue his presence, and the petition based on His promises, we will find our hearts satisfied with His presence and moves us to pray without ceasing.

CHAPTER XI
TESTIMONY FROM DAVID

1 **Samuel 17: 26-45**

26 David asked the men who were standing near him, 'What would be the reward for killing this Philistine and saving Israel from disgrace? **Who is this uncircumcised Philistine, to challenge the armies of the living God?'**

27 The people told him what they had been saying, 'That would be the reward for killing him,' they said.

28 His eldest brother Eliab heard David talking to the men and grew angry with him. 'Why have you come down here?' he said. 'Whom have you left in charge of those few sheep in the desert? I know how impudent and artful you are; you have come to watch the battle!'

29 David retorted, 'What have I done? May I not even speak?'

30 And he turned away from him to someone else and asked the same question, to which the people replied as before.

31 David's words were noted, however, and reported to Saul, who sent for him.

32 David said to Saul, 'Let no one be discouraged on his account; your servant will go and fight this Philistine.'

33 Saul said to David, 'You cannot go and fight the Philistine; you are only a boy and he has been a warrior since his youth.'

^{34} *David said to Saul, 'Your servant used to look after the sheep for his father and whenever a lion or a bear came and took a sheep from the flock,*

^{35} *I used to follow it up, lay into it and snatch the sheep out of its jaws. If it turned on me, I would seize it by the beard and batter it to death.*

^{36} ***Your servant has killed both lion and bear, and this uncircumcised Philistine will end up like one of them for having challenged the armies of the living God.'***

^{37} ***'Yahweh,' David went on, 'who delivered me from the claws of lion and bear, will deliver me from the clutches of this Philistine.' Then Saul said to David, 'Go, and Yahweh be with you!'***

^{38} *Saul dressed David in his own armour; he put a bronze helmet on his head, dressed him in a breastplate*

^{39} *and buckled his own sword over David's armour. David tried to walk but, not being used to them, said to Saul, 'I cannot walk in these; I am not used to them.' So they took them off again.*

^{40} *He took his stick in his hand, selected five smooth stones from the river bed and put them in his shepherd's bag, in his pouch; then, sling in hand, he walked towards the Philistine.*

^{41} *The Philistine, preceded by his shield-bearer, came nearer and nearer to David.*

^{42} *When the Philistine looked David up and down, what he saw filled him with scorn, because David was only a lad, with ruddy cheeks and an attractive appearance.*

^{43} *The Philistine said to David, 'Am I a dog for you to come after me with sticks?' And the Philistine cursed David by his gods.*

^{44} *The Philistine said to David, 'Come over here and I will give your flesh to the birds of the air and the wild beasts!'*

45 David retorted to the Philistine, 'You come to me with sword, spear and scimitar, but I come to you in the name of Yahweh Sabaoth, God of the armies of Israel, whom you have challenged.

As we read as above, we noticed that David really love and devote God dearly. David really had 100% FAITH to God. He loved and honoured to God with all his heart.

On the battlefield, when Goliath brazenly blasphemed God, David could not bear to hear the giant speak ill of God; he asked indignantly,

"Who is this uncircumcised Philistine that he should defy the armies of the living God?" 1 Samuel 17:26.

The mighty trained warriors had the nerve to silence Goliath, yet David in spite of his youth and lack of military training, readily stood up for God and took the giant Goliath head on.

We can read in 1 Samuel 17:36; "Your servant has killed both lions and bears; this uncircumcised Philistine shall be like one of them, David told Saul".

David was passionate for God. He cared greatly for God's glory and honour than his dear life. So his Faith was really genuine and 100 %. He placed God at the centre of his lives.

David was confident that God would deliver him from the giant Goliath's hand just as God had rescued him from fierce animals on several occasions in the past.

So David's faith to God is 100% as we read on 1 Samuel 17:27,

"The Lord, who saved me from the paw of the lion and from the paw of the bear, will save me from the hand of this Philistine".

David has a great relation with God, David trust God 100 %.

David seemed insignificant even in his father's eyes, but there was something that God noticed in David's heart which pleased God.

God told Samuel that He does not see as mortals see; they look on the outward appearance, but God looks on the heart (1 Samuel 16:7).

God overlooked David's tender age and instead focused on his heart and knew that this young had the potential and the requisite qualities to be the future king of Israel.

What about us?

Do we genuinely care about the sheep, care of the vulnerable people God has placed in our lives?

Are we like good shepherds to them, protecting them, guiding them, lending a listening ear when they need us or helping them in their spiritual growth?

How do we react when we encounter Goliaths unexpectedly in our lives, such as a financial crisis, bushfire, flood, relationship problems, Covid 19 or other health complications?

When our faith is tested, do we despair, or do we display trust as David did; that with the Lord's help we will conquer and defeat these giants plaguing us?

We need to have a BIGGER FAITH, when our problem is getting BIGGER as well.

First David had to encounter LION, then BEAR and then GOLIATH. His enemy was getting BIGGER and BIGGER, so his FAITH had to be BIGGER and BIGGER as well.

We need to have "a growing Faith to our Lord" as well, to get ready to encounter any issues. As children of our heavenly God, may we also cultivate an attitude like David who said,

"I keep the Lord always before me; because he is at my right hand, I shall not be moved" (Psalms 16: 8)

Once again, God is looking at the condition of our hearts.

CHAPTER XII
TESTIMONY FROM JABEZ

1 **Chronicles 4: 9-10**

⁹ Jabez was better known than his brothers. His mother gave him the name Jabez, 'because', she said, 'in distress I gave birth to him.'

¹⁰ Jabez called on the God of Israel. 'If you truly bless me,' he said, 'you will extend my lands, your hand will be with me, you will keep harm away and my distress will cease.' God granted him what he had asked.

As we know Scripture has many examples of prayers which we will teach us to depend and trust on God and call upon Him. We know that all Scripture is God-breathed and is useful for teaching, rebuking, and training in righteousness, so that we may be thoroughly equipped for every good work.

The prayer of Jabez is very inspiring and challenging for how he approached God with his requests.

Jabez was not using prayer as a formula to get something from God, rather He was calling upon God to help him accomplish the promises of God.

Let's see how this Jabez's prayer can be applied today as we seek God's provision and leading in our lives.

The Prayer of Jabez, 1 Chronicles 4: 9-10, we are learning:

1. Verse 9:

The name Jabez literally means "born with pain". His own mother named him this because of the pain she endured in labour.

When Jabez prays, he speaks against the testimony of his name and lets go of the shame it covered him in.

Learning for us: When we pray, we can come to God vulnerable and ready for Him to turn our weakness into His glory.

2. Verse 10:

This Scripture tells us about Jabez is that he cried to the God of Israel. Jabez states God's lordship and headship over his life.

Learning for us: When we pray, we begin by acknowledging who God is.

3. Verse 10: Then Jabez asked God to bless him". Jabez was not only recognizes God as the one and only true God, he also acknowledges that blessings come from God alone.

Learning for us: Are we chasing broken promises and blessings that the world tries to entice us with? Are we striving toward prosperity on our own strength? During our pray, please do it with a heart fully invested in the blessings of God and God Only.

4. Verse 10: Then Jabez asked God to multiply his territory. Some people may think that Jabez is simply referring to physical land when asking to multiply territory. But if we look at the condition of Jabez we can understand that he is not merely speaking in physical terms of wealth and prosperity.

But he asked in terms of impacting the kingdom of God. He wanted his spiritual territory to increase, to claim generations for the Lord of Israel.

Learning for us: When we pray, ask God to multiply your spiritual territory and to do more through you as well.

5. Verse 10: Then Jabez asked God's hand was with him. He wanted God to be in every minutes always with him. He understood the power of God's hand to protect and to lead in the right direction.

Blessings will become curses if it is not God's hand providing and guiding.

Learning for us: When we pray, request more than blessings and provision but that God's hand would lead you through any circumstances and trials that come your way.

6. Verse 10: Then he asked God to keep him away from any harm.

Learning for us: When we pray, please ask that our God would not lead us into temptation, but deliver us from evil and draw us closer to Yourself God.

CHAPTER XIII
TESTIMONY FROM JOB

Now, we are learning to pray with Job for guidance in prayer. Job is the story of a man who had it all and lost it all, a man who suffered greatly but never turned his back on God. On the other hand, it is also the story of a man who can teach us at several valuable lessons in prayer:

1. Pray what's really on your mind and in your heart:

Job was a blunt person, he didn't mince words with God. His prayers may seem unusual to many person. He said things like,

"I will give free rein to my complaint and speak out in the bitterness of my soul"

(Job 1:2).

Another day, he prayed,

"Stop frightening me with your terrors" (Job 13:21). He complained, *"Surely, O God, you have worn me out" (Job 16:7).*

He didn't hold back. He didn't hold forth platitudes.

If you want to pray like Job, you will pray with your true thoughts and feelings. God sees and knows those things anyway.

2. Ask God to speak:

In most occasion, Job repeatedly asked God to speak, he was praying things like,

"Tell me what charges you have against me" (Job 1:2) and

"Show me my offense" (Job 13:23).

Those are not a humble prayers of course, but too often in prayer we do all the talking.

We want God to listen to us but we seldom or never listen to Him and miss so much. We missed not only correction but also affirmation and guidance, among other things. So pray like Job, meaning Ask God to speak to you.

We can ask God to speak with a polite wording as well of course.

1. Keep asking:

When we read Job's book, sometimes we get weary of the back-and-forth between him and God and between him and his friends. But the learning which we can get from Job is Job's persistence.

He becomes more desperate as the story progresses, but he never gives up.

4. Accept correction:

Throughout the book that bears his name, Job repeatedly asks God to speak, to answer him. Job wanted God to answer him, but when God finally speaks, He says:

[4] Listen, please, and let me speak: I am going to ask the questions, and you are to inform me.

[5] Before, I knew you only by hearsay but now, having seen you with my own eyes,

[6] I retract what I have said, and repent in dust and ashes. [7] When Yahweh had finished saying this to Job, he said to Eliphaz of Teman, 'I burn with anger against you and your two friends, for not having spoken correctly about me as my servant Job has done.

As we read as above Job 42: 4-7, finally Job, bowed low and accepted God's correction. So be like Job and accept correction when God offers it, God gave Job everything back and doubled it as well (Job 42:10).

5. Wait A Little Longer:

In the midst of his gut-wrenching, life-changing trial, Job's wife encouraged him to "curse God and die" (Job 2:9).

But he did neither.

For 40 more chapters, he cried out to God, complained to God and even got petulant with God. But he waited and he endured. And eventually, the Bible says:

"The Lord blessed the latter part of Job's life more than the first" (Job 42: 10-12.

Learning to us: We can pray like Job if you want to. Go ahead and cry and moan and lay it all out. But wait a little longer as well.

Because that God's time zone is different than us. God may not show up according to our schedule, because sometimes the waiting is as much a part of His plan for you as the destination as well.

CHAPTER XIV
TESTIMONY FROM ISAIAH

I SAIAH 64: 1-4

1 as fire sets brushwood alight, as fire makes water boil—to make your name known to your foes; the nations would tremble at your presence,

2 at the unexpected miracles you would do. (Oh, that you would come down, in your presence the mountains would quake!)

3 Never has anyone heard, no ear has heard, no eye has seen any god but you act like this for the sake of those who trust him.

4 You come to meet those who are happy to act uprightly; keeping your ways reminds them of you. Yes, you have been angry and we have been sinners; now we persist in your ways and we shall be saved.

As we read as above, in Isaiah 64, we found one of the most remarkable prayers of intercession recorded in the Bible.

Where the prophet calls upon the Lord, saying, 'Oh, that you would rend the heavens and come down, that the mountains might quake at your presence ',

"As fire kindles the brushwood, as fire causes water to boil '"

To make your name known to your adversaries that the nations may tremble at your presence!' we can read in Isaiah 64, verses 1-2.

As we know the word 'rend' means to tear open. Isaiah was crying out to God that He would 'tear open' the heavens and show Himself to the world so that the world might see Him as Isaiah had seen Him.

We believe that Isaiah was reflecting on a previous experience in his life, as in Isaiah 6:1-8, he had been caught up into heaven and received the anointing for his life and prophetic ministry.

He recalls it, saying, 'In the year that King Uzziah died, I saw also the Lord seated on a throne, high and exalted, and the train of his robe filled the temple' (Isaiah 6:1).

Isaiah continued to describe his experience in God's presence. He spoke of angelic beings around the throne crying out, 'Holy, holy, holy, is the Lord Almighty; the whole earth is full of his glory' (Isaiah 6: 3).

He spoke of the visible manifestation of God's glory. He described his sudden and overwhelming awareness of sin when he stood in the magnificent presence of the holiness of God.

Pay careful attention to what the angels were crying to one another. Notice, they did not say, 'Heaven is full of his glory.' Rather, they said, 'The earth is full of his glory.' This was a prophetic insight into a time that is coming.

When Isaiah prayed for God to rend the heavens and come down, he was asking for the fulfilment of the prophetic promise he had received in his vision many years earlier.

He was saying in essence, 'Lord, if the earth is going to be filled with your glory, you must rend the heavens and come down!'

Isaiah realised that this 'rending of the heavens' would be necessary for God to fulfil His plan for this world.

As we all knew, the prayer of Isaiah was answered 2,000 years ago! God truly did rend the heavens and came down through Jesus Christ.

Learning for us: God has rent the heavens and has come down. He has destroyed that ancient barrier between heaven and earth, and today all the riches and resources of God are available to the one who will take them by faith through prayer.

Knowing that God has already destroyed everything that stands between Him and us by the blood of Jesus Christ. He truly has given us the keys to the Kingdom of Heaven.

Isaiah's prayer was answered. The Lord came down. He became a man! He became one of us! He came in person for us!

CHAPTER XV
TESTIMONY FROM JEREMIAH

J eremiah 33: 1-4

¹ Jeremiah was still confined to the Court of the Guard when the word of Yahweh came to him a second time, as follows,

² 'Yahweh who made the earth, who formed it and set it firm— Yahweh is his name—says this,

³ "Call to me and I will answer you; I will tell you great secrets of which you know nothing.

⁴ For this is what Yahweh, God of Israel, says about the houses of this city and the palaces of the kings of Judah which are about to be destroyed by means of the earthworks and the sword;

The prophet Jeremiah was not a popular man, because he was telling a truth. He declared the truth God had given to him, that Judah would soon start 70 long years in captivity, then the people threw him into prison.

With this situation, Jeremiah learned something profound about prayer. In Jeremiah 33:1–4 says, While Jeremiah was still confined in the courtyard of the guard, the word of the LORD came to him a second time:

"This is what the LORD says, he who made the earth, the LORD who formed it and established it—the LORD is his name: 'Call to me and I will answer you and tell you great and unsearchable things you do not know.

Prayer is a very real part of a vital relationship with our God. It is not reserved for some special spiritual elite, but it is for us. Learning for us from the prophet Jeremiah, which will transform our old notions about prayer into something fresh and new:

1. God says, "Call to me."

He wants to hear from you. His loving, almighty heart desires to hear your inner thoughts and feelings. He wants to hear from you in the hard times and how your life is going as a daily basis. In fact, we can pray simply to praise, worship and give thanks for what he has done to us.

2. God says, "I will answer you."

How good is this? What is your thoughts? Perhaps you asked God for something he did not give you, and since then you have thought secret worries that he did not hear or did not care to answer.

But God himself says to you,

"I will answer you."

That answer may not take the form you anticipate or come when you desire, but he will respond. He might say "yes," "no," or "wait." You may not understand the reasons behind His answer, but you can trust that it is best for you in the long run.

3. God says that he will "tell you great and unsearchable things you do not know."

God is Our Creator, we have finite wisdom and understanding; God knows all. He knows the big picture; you see merely a tiny piece. When you ask him to guide you, he works to direct you as a part of his higher vision and calling.

Learning for us: If we take that first step of calling out to him, prayer can become an important part of a dynamic relationship with almighty God.

Why not we do it today?

CHAPTER XVI
TESTIMONY FROM DANIEL

D aniel 9: 1-11

¹ It was the first year of Darius son of Artaxerxes, a Mede by race who assumed the throne of Chaldaea.

² In the first year of his reign I, Daniel, was studying the scriptures, counting over the number of years—as revealed by Yahweh to the prophet¹ Jeremiah² —that were to pass before the desolation of Jerusalem³ would come to an end, namely seventy years.

³ I turned my face to the Lord⁴ God⁵ begging for time⁶ to pray and to plead, with fasting, sackcloth and ashes.

⁴ I pleaded with Yahweh my God⁷ and made this confession: 'O my Lord, God⁸ great and to be feared, you keep the covenant and show faithful love towards those who love you and who observe your commandments:

---

1.   https://www.catholic.org/encyclopedia/view.php?id=9674

2.   https://www.catholic.org/bible/book.php?id=30

3.   https://www.catholic.org/encyclopedia/view.php?id=6304

4.   https://www.catholic.org/encyclopedia/view.php?id=5217

5.   https://www.catholic.org/encyclopedia/view.php?id=5217

6.   https://www.catholic.org/encyclopedia/view.php?id=11571

7.   https://www.catholic.org/encyclopedia/view.php?id=5217

8.   https://www.catholic.org/encyclopedia/view.php?id=5217

⁵ we have sinned, we have done wrong, we have acted wickedly, and we have betrayed your commandments and rulings and turned away from them.

⁶ We have not listened to your servants the prophets, who spoke in your name to our kings, our chief men, our ancestors and all people of the country.

⁷ Saving justice, Lord, is yours; we have only the look of shame we wear today, we, the people of Judah, the inhabitants of Jerusalem, the whole of Israel, near and far away, in every country to which you have dispersed us because of the treachery we have committed against you.

⁸ To us, our kings, our chief men and our ancestors, belongs the look of shame, O Yahweh, since we have sinned against you.

⁹ And it is for the Lord⁹ our God¹⁰ to have mercy and to pardon, since we have betrayed him,

¹⁰ and have not listened to the voice of Yahweh our God¹¹ nor followed the laws he has given us through his servants the prophets.

¹¹ The whole of Israel has flouted your Law¹² and turned away, unwilling to listen to your voice; and the curse and imprecation written in the Law¹³ of Moses, the servant of God, have come pouring down on us, because we have sinned against him.

Daniel's prayer was prompted by reading God's Word as we read in Daniel 9, verses 1–3. Daniel had been reading the words of the prophet Jeremiah, words of the Lord given to Jeremiah", in Daniel 9, verse 2.

---

9. *https://www.catholic.org/encyclopedia/view.php?id=5217*

10. *https://www.catholic.org/encyclopedia/view.php?id=5217*

11. *https://www.catholic.org/encyclopedia/view.php?id=5217*

12. *https://www.catholic.org/encyclopedia/view.php?id=6916*

13. *https://www.catholic.org/encyclopedia/view.php?id=6916*

As He read the Book of Jeremiah, he found in it that the Jerusalem's desolation would last seventy years. The passages that he was pondering were in Jeremiah 29, verses 10 – 14, as follows:

10 For Yahweh[14] says this: When the seventy years granted to Babylon are over, I shall intervene on your behalf and fulfil my favourable promise to you by bringing you back to this place.

11 Yes, I know what plans I have in mind[15] for you, Yahweh[16] declares, plans for peace, not for disaster, to give you a future and a hope.

12 When you call to me and come and pray to me, I shall listen to you.13 When you search for me, you will[17] find me; when you search wholeheartedly for me

,14 I shall let you find me (Yahweh declares. I shall restore your fortunes and gather you in from all the nations and wherever I have driven you, Yahweh[18] declares. I shall bring you back to the place from which I exiled you).

In these oracles, Jeremiah told that the Lord planned to subject his people to Babylon for seventy years for their sin, but at the end of that time, God would act to judge the Babylonians and to bring his people home.

Even though it wasn't quite seventy years yet since the destruction of Judah, Daniel began to pray to fulfil of the second half of this prophecy: the gracious restoration of God's people to his land as declared by God to Jeremiah in Jeremiah 29, verses 10-11.

---

14.   *https://www.catholic.org/encyclopedia/view.php?id=6291*

15.   *https://www.catholic.org/encyclopedia/view.php?id=8001*

16.   *https://www.catholic.org/encyclopedia/view.php?id=6291*

17.   *https://www.catholic.org/encyclopedia/view.php?id=12332*

18.   *https://www.catholic.org/encyclopedia/view.php?id=6291*

We learn that Daniel was not merely praying for his comfort, but he prayed for God's people and God's kingdom. It is okay if we ask for,

"Give us this day our daily bread," but we must also remember to pray,

"Your kingdom come, your will be done, on earth as it is in heaven", as well.

We learn from Daniel:

1. Daniel's practice of praying:

We can read in Daniel 6, his practice of praying was three times a day as a regular basis and as his longstanding practice as well. He was formed by his reading of the Scripture and learned from Jeremiah.

2. Three of Daniel's prayer: conjuration, confession, and petition

We noticed that there are three aspects of Daniel's prayer, which are conjuration, confession, and petition.

He began by recognizing and acknowledging who God is (conjuration); then he confessed the sins of his community and acknowledged the rightness of God's judgment upon them (confession), and he pled with God to fulfil his purposes for his people (petition).

So when we pray, we should begin by reminding ourselves of God's greatness and his grace, shown in his faithfulness to his covenant promises.

Why we are praying?

We pray because of our God's grace. So do not forget of our God's greatness when we are praying.

Regarding to our sin, we do not want to brush it under the carpet and pretend that it doesn't exist. See in Daniel's prayer.

Please remember God's grace and to confess our sin before him, ask on his sovereign mercy. When we recognize our God's greatness and His Grace, it will regularly drive us to our knees in thanksgiving and confession and passionate for our petition for the sake of Our Lord name as well.

3. Daniel learned from Jeremiah

As Daniel learned from Jeremiah, of course we can learn from Daniel as well or learn from others Special Person, as we can read in our Bible. Especially we can learn from Our Lord, Jesus Christ, The Only Son of Our God.

We can learn to powerfully pray like Daniel by studying his own prayer. Daniel recognized and acknowledged at the outset the God to whom his prayer was addressed.

CHAPTER XVII

TESTIMONY FROM THE APOSTLE PAUL

Philippians 3: 7 -21

7But what were once my assets I now through Christ[1] Jesus[2] count as losses.

8 Yes, I will[3] go further: because of the supreme advantage of knowing Christ[4] Jesus[5] my Lord, I count everything else as loss. For him I have accepted the loss of all other things, and look on them all as filth if only I can gain Christ

9 and be given a place in him, with the uprightness I have gained not from the Law, but through faith[6] in Christ, an uprightness from God, based on faith,

10 that I may come to know him and the power of his resurrection, and partake of his sufferings by being moulded to the pattern of his death,

11 striving towards the goal of resurrection from the dead.

---

1. *https://www.catholic.org/clife/jesus*

2. *https://www.catholic.org/clife/jesus*

3. *https://www.catholic.org/encyclopedia/view.php?id=12332*

4. *https://www.catholic.org/clife/jesus*

5. *https://www.catholic.org/clife/jesus*

6. *https://www.catholic.org/encyclopedia/view.php?id=4554*

[12] *Not that I have secured it already, nor yet reached my goal, but I am still pursuing it in the attempt to take hold of the prize for which Christ[7] Jesus[8] took hold of me.*

[13] *Brothers, I do not reckon myself as having taken hold of it; I can only say that forgetting all that lies behind me, and straining forward to what lies in front,*

[14] *I am racing towards the finishing-point to win the prize of God's heavenly call in Christ[9] Jesus.*

[15] *So this is the way in which all of us who are mature should be thinking, and if you are still thinking differently in any way, then God[10] has yet to make this matter[11] clear to you.*

[16] *Meanwhile, let us go forward from the point we have each attained.*

[17] *Brothers, be united in imitating me. Keep your eyes fixed on those who act according to the example you have from me.*

[18] *For there are so many people of whom I have often warned you, and now I warn you again with tears in my eyes, who behave like the enemies of Christ's cross.*

[19] *They are destined to be lost; their god[12] is the stomach; they glory[13] in what they should think shameful, since their minds are set on earthly things.*

[20] *But our homeland is in heaven[14] and it is from there that we are expecting a Saviour, the Lord[15] Jesus[16] Christ,*

---

7. https://www.catholic.org/clife/jesus

8. https://www.catholic.org/clife/jesus

9. https://www.catholic.org/clife/jesus

10. https://www.catholic.org/encyclopedia/view.php?id=5217

11. https://www.catholic.org/encyclopedia/view.php?id=7732

12. https://www.catholic.org/encyclopedia/view.php?id=5217

13. https://www.catholic.org/encyclopedia/view.php?id=5201

14. https://www.catholic.org/encyclopedia/view.php?id=5593

15. https://www.catholic.org/encyclopedia/view.php?id=5217

[21] who will[17] transfigure the wretched body of ours into the mould of his glorious body, through the working of the power which he has, even to bring all things under his mastery.

As we can read in Philippians 3, verses 7 – 21 as above, we agree that Paul was an extraordinary man and an inspirational man of God and we learn of so many things from him.

He was named as Saul, he killed so many Christians in so many years as well. He did everything that he could to stop the growth of Christianity. But after he had an encounter with the Lord, he changed his ways, his name, and his heart, as we read in Acts 9, verses 1-19:

[1] Meanwhile Saul[18] was still breathing threats to slaughter the Lord's disciples. He went to the high priest

[2] and asked for letters addressed to the synagogues in Damascus, that would authorise him to arrest and take to Jerusalem[19] any followers of the Way, men or women, that he might find.

[3] It happened that while he was travelling to Damascus[20] and approaching the city, suddenly a light from heaven[21] shone all round him.

[4] He fell to the ground, and then he heard a voice saying, 'Saul, Saul, why are you persecuting me?

[5] 'Who are you, Lord?' he asked, and the answer came, 'I am Jesus, whom you are persecuting.

[6] Get up and go into the city, and you will[22] be told what you are to do.'

---

16.   *https://www.catholic.org/clife/jesus*

17.   *https://www.catholic.org/encyclopedia/view.php?id=12332*

18.   *https://www.catholic.org/encyclopedia/view.php?id=10518*

19.   *https://www.catholic.org/encyclopedia/view.php?id=6304*

20.   *https://www.catholic.org/encyclopedia/view.php?id=3633*

21.   *https://www.catholic.org/encyclopedia/view.php?id=5593*

22.   *https://www.catholic.org/encyclopedia/view.php?id=12332*

[7] *The men travelling with Saul[23] stood there speechless, for though they heard the voice they could see no one.*

[8] *Saul got up from the ground, but when he opened his eyes he could see nothing at all, and they had to lead him into Damascus[24] by the hand.*

[9] *For three days he was without his sight and took neither food nor drink.*

[10] *There was a disciple[25] in Damascus[26] called Ananias, and he had a vision in which the Lord[27] said to him, 'Ananias!' When he replied, 'Here I am, Lord,'*

[11] *the Lord[28] said, 'Get up and go to Straight Street and ask at the house of Judas for someone called Saul, who comes from Tarsus. At this moment he is praying,*

[12] *and has seen a man[29] called Ananias coming in and laying hands on him to give him back his sight.'*

[13] *But in response, Ananias said, 'Lord, I have heard from many people about this man[30] and all the harm he has been doing to your holy people in Jerusalem.*

[14] *He has come here with a warrant from the chief priests to arrest everybody who invokes your name.'*

[15] *The Lord[31] replied, 'Go, for this man[32] is my chosen instrument to bring my name before gentiles[33] and kings[34] and before the people of Israel;*

---

23.   *https://www.catholic.org/encyclopedia/view.php?id=10518*

24.   *https://www.catholic.org/encyclopedia/view.php?id=3633*

25.   *https://www.catholic.org/encyclopedia/view.php?id=3895*

26.   *https://www.catholic.org/encyclopedia/view.php?id=3633*

27.   *https://www.catholic.org/encyclopedia/view.php?id=5217*

28.   *https://www.catholic.org/encyclopedia/view.php?id=5217*

29.   *https://www.catholic.org/encyclopedia/view.php?id=7463*

30.   *https://www.catholic.org/encyclopedia/view.php?id=7463*

31.   *https://www.catholic.org/encyclopedia/view.php?id=5217*

[16] I myself will[35] show him how much he must suffer for my name.'

[17] Then Ananias went. He entered the house, and laid his hands on Saul[36] and said, 'Brother Saul, I have been sent by the Lord[37] Jesus, who appeared to you on your way here, so that you may recover your sight and be filled with the Holy Spirit.'[18] It was as though scales fell away from his eyes and immediately he was able to see again. So he got up and was baptised,

[19] and after taking some food he regained his strength. After he had spent only a few days with the disciples in Damascus,

Then he started preaching the Word of the Lord and he brought so many people to the Kingdom of the Our Lord.

He wrote a lot in the New Testament, such as Paul's Letter to the Romans, to the Corinthians, to the Galatians, to the Ephesians, to the Philippians, to the Colossians, to the Thessalonians, to Timothy, to Titus, to Philemon as well.

Even though he was a murderer before, but he has changed totally and he was an example of someone who has a heart on fire for the Lord.

So why not we learn from him as well. There are several things:

1. No one is beyond the saving grace of God

As Christians, I do know that sometimes we can be really hard on ourselves for our mistakes. We think that if we mess up, Our Lord won't love us anymore. Paul killed so many Christian people in his past.

He tried to stop Christianity. But God forgave him, had a purpose for him, and loved him as well.

32.   *https://www.catholic.org/encyclopedia/view.php?id=7463*

33.   *https://www.catholic.org/encyclopedia/view.php?id=5057*

34.   *https://www.catholic.org/encyclopedia/view.php?id=6650*

35.   *https://www.catholic.org/encyclopedia/view.php?id=12332*

36.   *https://www.catholic.org/encyclopedia/view.php?id=10518*

37.   *https://www.catholic.org/encyclopedia/view.php?id=5217*

We are not perfect people because we live in a sin fallen world. It's impossible for us to be completely perfect, and that's why we need God in our lives. So we should not get discouraged by our mistakes, please allow God to transform and strengthen us.

God gave Paul grace and transformed him into a completely different person. Like Paul, God can do the same for us. So please do not abandon praying and have a good relation to our God, because we felt that we have sin.

2. Spend time with Jesus in praying

Paul wanted to know more and more of Jesus. He spent quality time with Him as often as he could. In Philippians 3 verses 10-11 as above, we read that Paul want to know Jesus Christ, to know the power of his resurrection and participation in His sufferings, becoming like Him in his death, and so attaining to the resurrection from the dead as well.

Paul knew that the only way that he would get to know God on the level that he wanted to was by spending time with Him in His Word and through prayer. Paul shows us the importance of quality time and that it results in knowing Christ intimately and personally.

3. Paul had a totally Faith to Jesus Christ in any situation

We read in Philippians 4:10-13:

10 As for me, I am full of joy in the Lord, now that at last your consideration for me has blossomed again; though I recognise that you really did have consideration before, but had no opportunity to show it.

11 I do not say this because I have lacked anything; I have learnt to manage with whatever I have.

12 I know how to live modestly, and I know how to live luxuriously too: in every way now I have mastered the secret[38] of all conditions: full stomach and empty stomach, plenty and poverty.

13 There is nothing I cannot do in the One who strengthens me.

Paul said,

---

38.   *https://www.catholic.org/encyclopedia/view.php?id=10643*

"I am not saying this because I am in need, for I have learned to be content whatever the circumstances. I know what it is to be in need, and I know what it is to have plenty.

I have learned the secret of being content in and in every situation, whether well fed or hungry, whether living in plenty or in want.

I can do all things through him who gives me strength. Paul's secret of the contentment was that he drew his strength from the Jesus Christ.

He learned to rely on God's promises and strength to help him be content in any situation. He had a total Faith that Jesus would supply him with everything that he would need, no matter what.

As Christian, we tend to be the type of person who always worries, and we know that this is a very difficult thing to accomplish. But if we follow Paul by draw our strength from Jesus Christ as well, it is possible for us to accomplish this.

4. Paul stand firm in Jesus Christ

Please read in Philippians 3:20-21 as above, Paul wrote,

"But our citizenship is in heaven. We eagerly await a Saviour from there, the Lord Jesus Christ, who, by the power that enables him to bring everything under his control, will transform our lowly bodies so that they will be like his glorious body."

The way to stand firm is to keep our eyes on Him.

It can become so easy for us to be distracted by everything going on around us, but we need to remember that this world is not our home. Standing firm means to resist the ways of this world.

Don't get discouraged or lose heart when you mess up, but instead continue to press into the Lord. He promises strength, so with Him, you can stay true to the Lord.

That are just some few points that we can learn from Paul. Of course there are so much more that we can learn from Paul.

Jesus Christ, our Lord used a man who had a lot of sin but Jesus transformed him into A SUPER Evangelistic Person.

In all of these points that we can learn from Paul, Jesus Christ has a purpose for us as well, and with Jesus Christ's strength, Jesus Christ can use us to do great things for His kingdom and glory.

CHAPTER XVIII
CONCLUSION

As we have discussed in Chapter I, to become A Truly Prayer, minimum we need to have 4 things, which are:

1. Attention
2. Devotion
3. Faith
4. And Forego

When we pray we have to pay attention for what we are saying and should be saying it with love, faith and forego as well on the same time.

And there are five types of prayer in the tradition of the Church, as follows:

1. Worship and Adoration
2. Intercession
3. Petition
4. Thanksgiving
5. Praise

We have read a lot of Testimonies from The Old Testament as well as from "Our Today World", which we can make the conclusion of Where, What, When, Who, Why and HOW the prayers got answered.

We knew that there are several condition to get prayer answered. We believe that conclusion will have some relation as we discussed on Chapter I as above.

Now, I would like you to see the other side of the Testimonies of The Prayers Answered from The New Testament as follows:

A. Please read in Luke 5, verses 12-13:

Now it happened that Jesus[1] was in one of the towns when suddenly a man[2] appeared, covered with a skin-disease. Seeing Jesus[3] he fell on his face and implored him saying, 'Sir, if you are <u>willing</u> you can cleanse me.

'He stretched out his hand, and touched him saying, 'I am <u>willing</u>. Be cleansed.' At once the skin-disease left him.

The very important WORD of this verses is **WILLING**, that man who got a skin-disease besides he truly had 100 % Faith/ Devotion to Jesus (by fell on his face and implored) has asked Jesus about **HIS WILLING** to do something to him or not. Meaning that man let Jesus to make A CALL, not that man call!

B. Please read in Luke 22, verse 42:

'Father,' he said, 'if you are <u>willing</u>, take this cup away from me. Nevertheless, let your will[4] <u>be done, not mine.</u>'

I believe that you remember the background of this narratives, Jesus was going to the Cross. Jesus prayed to His Father whether "His Father are **willing** to cancel the original plan", but Jesus let His Father to make The Call for Jesus.

C. Please read in 1 John 4 verse 8:

Whoever fails to love does not know God, because God[5] is love'.

So Our Father is Love, He love us 100 %, because He created us. Jesus in "The Lord Prayer", to call His Father as OUR FATHER as well. So we are OUR FATHER's children. Once again Our Father love us 100 %, His Creation, His Children.

---

1.   *https://www.catholic.org/clife/jesus*

2.   *https://www.catholic.org/encyclopedia/view.php?id=7463*

3.   *https://www.catholic.org/clife/jesus*

4.   https://www.catholic.org/encyclopedia/view.php?id=12332

5.   https://www.catholic.org/encyclopedia/view.php?id=5217

It does not means that OUR FATHER always give us what we ask for. Not giving everything to children is happened in Human Life. We know that a child asked something, but his/her parent said NO to him/her. Because the parent knew a better options. Even though the child cried, but if the parent love the child, the parent still did not give the child what he/she asked for, if it was not suitable for the child. So our parent did not give to us everything for what we asked for. OUR FATHER did not take "this cup away" from Jesus as well, HIS SON, even though Jesus asked for.

OUR FATHER is THE GREAT CREATOR for human and universe. He is our Almighty God, He know much better than us as a human being (His Creation). He think everything for the sake of us and for long term purpose. So we can't say that Our Lord never listen to us as His Creation.

Why not we follow Jesus by saying:

YOUR WILL BE DONE, NOT MINE

Every time when we pray!

D. But we keep praying and asking:

With all consideration as above from Chapter I until now, with all testimonies from The Old Testament, from The New Testament and from "Our Today's World", we knew that Our Father answered prayers. So we keep praying and asking, with the faith and hope that OUR LORD will make it happens, **if HE IS WILLING!**

*Let we pray The Lord Prayer again:

Our Father,
Who art in Heaven,
Hallowed be Thy Name.
Thy Kingdom come,
Thy will be done on earth
As it is in Heaven.
Give us this day our daily bread,
And forgive us our trespasses,
As we forgive those who trespass against us,
And lead us not into temptation,
But deliver us from evil.
Amen

* Or in Latin, Pater Noster:

PATER noster,
qui es in cœlis;
sanctificetur nomen tuum:
Adveniat regnum tuum;
fiat voluntas tua, sicut in cœlo,
et in terra.
Panem nostrum cotidianum
da nobis hodie:
Et dimitte nobis debita nostra,
sicut et nos dimittimus
debitoribus nostris:
et nc nos inducas

in tentationem:
sed libera nos a malo.

Don't miss out!

Visit the website below and you can sign up to receive emails whenever The Blessed Creation publishes a new book. There's no charge and no obligation.

https://books2read.com/r/B-A-XGAX-AJVFC

BOOKS 2 READ

Connecting independent readers to independent writers.

Also by The Blessed Creation

How to Pray a Good Prayer and Simple Guide for Normal People and Get Answered (With Testimonies)
Panda Panda Bear What Do You Learn: With Jokes and Quizzes
Little David Learns to Earn a Lot of Money

About the Author

ABOUT THE AUTHOR

The Blessed Creation is The Home of one Family with several persons. All Family Members grew a passion to empower people to live life to the fullest. We believe that everyone has the opportunity to get the right support around them.

The Blessed Creation believe that we will empower people for BETTER LIFE by sharing stories through publishing the great and awesome books. It is a GIFT to the WORLD.

Everyone has biggest passion about writing and creation for everything which are very good to share to the World. One of us is a freelance editor, has a Graduate Certificate of Editing and Publishing. This person has biggest passion to get perfecting book manuscripts for publication. He is passionate about art, including how to make beautiful book to share.

We have several artist who thinking outside the square and giving us a lot of ideas for our potential Buyers to enjoy.

Want to contact us ? Just drop an email to: theblessedcreation17@gmail.com